514 715

MAN-TALK

Prayers for the Man at Work

———◆———

Jim Daughdrill, Jr.

HARPER & ROW, PUBLISHERS
New York : Evanston : San Francisco : London

FIRST EDITION

STANDARD BOOK NUMBER: 06–061698–9

LIBRARY OF CONGRESS CATALOG CARD NUMBER: 72–78048

Designed by C. Linda Dingler

CONTENTS

SUMMER

FALL

WINTER

INTRODUCTION

The idea for this book began to germinate on a rainy night six years ago. I was a seminarian. Previously I had been in the textile business for eight years, five as president of a carpet manufacturing corporation and its subsidiary companies. I knew the tensions and concerns of businessmen.

On that particular rainy evening, I met with fifteen business executives in Atlanta, to discuss our common concern: *How do you live your faith on the job?*

As the rain poured down outside, one man after another echoed, "It helps when we talk about my faith and my job on Sunday nights, but where do I get help Monday through Friday?"

We decided to look.

During the next week we found plenty of "faith-boosters" for women and families. There were many "apron inspirations," and "mealtime meditations." But aids for the Christian businessman at work? Nothing.

So we started our own program. I wrote devotionals for three months. Each was printed on a 3 by 7 card, with an hourly appointment calendar on the back. We mailed these cards—one for each day of the work week—timed to arrive first thing every Monday morning.

We named the program "My Vocation Is My Ministry."

It caught on quickly. Men gave their cards to other businessmen who asked to be put on the mailing list. Requests came that friends and associates be added to the list. Often, unsolicited gifts were received. This helped to offset increasing costs of the mushrooming program. When I moved to another church, we started the mailings again —with the same gratifying results! During those six years, my files swelled with thoughtful letters from businessmen. Many of these were top executives of some of the nation's greatest corporations.

New prayers have been added as more and more men began to share their deep concerns with me. All the prayers have been read, discussed and *prayed* by men at work. Many have encouraged the publication of these messages for a wider audience. *Man—Talk* is the result.

I express my thanks to former associates in the textile business, men in the Young Presidents' Organization, and men of Northwest Presbyterian Church, Atlanta, and St. Andrew's, Little Rock. From their lives and their *man-talk* I have learned that each type of work can be a true ministry.

Jim Daughdrill

Atlanta, Georgia

SPRING

The Economy Would Be a Wreck!

"Go, sell your possessions and give to the poor.
. . . and come, follow Me."

Jesus, surely this doesn't mean *everybody*—
the economy would be a wreck! You called Abraham to
leave his country; Peter to
leave the fishing business; Paul to change completely. . .
What is your call to *me?*

Is it *just* as radical, but I'm not listening?
Do I expect too-little-change in my life and
my values? Am I *willing* to do what you say?

Maybe that's the key—*am* I willing—
to leave, to change radically, to expect great
discipleship?

God, whether you call me to "lay down my nets" and
follow
you, or "take up my work today" and follow you; make
me willing—*really* willing to do what you want.

Amen.

For the One Who Brought in Coffee

Thank you for unexpected joys! . . . for the one who
brought flowers to work . . . for the one who
brought in coffee . . . and for the one person
who noticed my new suit.

Thanks for the one who was firm with me when I
needed it
. . . for the unexpected phone call . . . the inner-office
memo that said "Thanks."

Lord, thank you for the conscious glimpse of you
through the day.

Amen.

Shuffling Papers, and Busywork

God, sometimes I shuffle papers for hours and make busy work because others *expect* me to be here and to be busy. Or maybe it's my own compulsion. When lulls come I wish I could go play golf, and come back better equipped to do the job . . . but I'd feel guilty because I wouldn't be playing the right part or acting the accepted role.

God, I'm afraid of having nothing to do—even for a few hours. We live by a formula that says to be important is to be busy. So I stay busy. I make busywork. I am uncomfortable when those around me are not busy.

Sometimes my prayers are busywork. I feel guilty when I'm not busy with you. God, help me to be *me*, and not the *role* I picture.

Amen.

When My Ears Get Pinned Back

God, I don't feel like praying now. I'm tired of taking the brunt of other people's problems! My ears get pinned back by customers—even when I'm not at fault! Pressures from their *own* companies get taken out on me!

And I have to take it when other people around here have personal problems! If we had plenty of time to talk things over it might be okay, but I've got a job to do—I'm no nursemaid!

Get 'em off my back, God. I've *had* it with their problems!

*   *   *

But God, thank you for listening to mine . . .

Amen.

We're Supposed To Be the Best

God, my company is supposed to be the best.
Do you believe that?

Sometimes I don't, and it's an empty feeling.
So much of my security seems to come from
unquestioned shallow enthusiasm.

It would be nice if all companies and
everyone could take down their guards. But
I can't do it if others won't! So, we go on
with pretenses, not trusting others, even though
we long to change.

God, enter our whirlpool. Redeem us, and give
us strength to redeem our relationships;
through Jesus Christ my Lord.

Amen.

I Don't Want To Get Involved

Heavenly Father, I know how to build a wall
around myself. I avoid deep personal conversations
with anyone at work, because I don't want to get
involved. It's wrong I know, but we can't over-
fraternize.

I end up being nice but not personal; near
but not close; friendly but not a friend.

Jesus didn't build walls—but it's sure
hard to follow his example. Help me to live
like him who was tempted like me; in his name.

Amen.

I Don't Know Where I'll Fit In

God, when I look at tomorrow I don't know
where I'll fit in. With competition, mergers,
new machines, my experience has questionable value.
I'm not getting any younger. I'm scared.

In the jostling between young ambition and
old experience, I may *not* fit in—I can't
demand it!

Grant me the strength to do the best I can,
trusting in you for life and the needs of tomorrow.

God, don't remove the risks. But give me the
strength that comes only to those who dare to
live for others. I pray for the peace that
passes understanding; through Christ my Lord.

Amen.

I Don't Feel Like Praying

God, thank you for your providence—
even on days when I don't feel like praying.

> Amen.

The Year Is One-Fourth Gone

God, the year is one-fourth gone. How time
flies! I feel drained with each month's
passing. Life seems less and less to be
a plan that I control. Grant me a new
awareness of your sovereignty.

*   *   *

And so I look to the future with new hope.
Help me to do my best; to know that my best
is limited; and to trust more fully in you.

Use me in showing your love to those who
do not know it; through Jesus Christ.

Amen.

My Convictions Don't Show

God, my convictions don't show. I am one of
the ones who'd rather not get involved. When
others fight injustice, I feel like it's not
my fight.

When some protest war, I try to believe
that they are weak, and I am brave . . . but
you and I know I'm not. God, my convictions
don't show.

Help me yield my convictions to you. Make
me humble and bold, free and dependent,
determined and yielded.

Mold my convictions that I may lose my life . . .
and find it . . . beginning *now*.

Amen.

Make Me a Good Receiver

God, I know it is more
blessed to give than to receive,
but it is harder for *me* to
receive. Help me to receive the
most important things in life—
the little things. Grant me
refreshment this week-end—
refreshment for my work and the
hurrying and demands that rob me
during the week.

Make me able to receive the
gifts of your creation. I want
to feel the beauty and order of
a walk in the woods, of sun on
my face, of budding leaves, and
laughter . . . of flickering fire-
light, worship, a touch, a song,
a renewed spirit; an awareness
of you.

Amen.

When I Have To Walk a Fine Line

God, I have to walk a fine line in my
work.

I have to be strong for others, even when
I don't feel like it. I have to be
enthusiastic for others even when I'm
discouraged.

I am lonesome. Responsibility for others
is not an easy weight to carry, and I can't
even talk to them about it!

I'm glad I can talk to you. Thank you.

Amen.

Things Change So Fast

Dear God, this time with you is like an
oasis in the desert. I know that all
time is in your hands, but it really
doesn't seem that way in the fret of
my work.

Things change so fast. Security is
short-lived. I work to bring about
change as much as anyone else, but I
am never really comfortable with it.
The unknown is harder than the familiar . . .
Jesus did not have a place to lay his
head; I think I know something about how He felt.

I'm glad he knows how I feel.

Amen.

Checks, Contracts, Memos

Many people know me only by what I write, or what
I sign. Give me sensitivity and an understanding
of those to whom I write.

How important the pen has been in history!
Martin Luther, John Hancock, Shakespeare,
Adolf Hitler, Moses, Paul . . . how important
it is to my work today!——checks, contracts,
purchase orders, memos.

God, help me to use this power for you.
May I write in love; and sign in truth.
I ask this in the name of Him who said,
"I am the Truth."

Amen.

People-Goals

God, I live many days without a direction. I just react to whatever comes up.

Help me to set some goals—not just for more profit, more business, or higher efficiency—but "people-goals."

By the end of this year what should have happened in the lives of the people here?

How can each person's work be made more fulfilling (to him and the company)?

How can we become better acquainted?

What can I do to be more concerned about people?

God, help me to set some goals.

Amen.

I Hardly Notice My Desk Light

It lights my work. It brightens
dark days. I notice it most on dark days.
On pretty days I hardly seem to notice it.

*   *   *

God, I am that way with you. When things
are dark I want to feel your nearness most, because
I need you most. When things go right for me,
I forget you. Forgive me for thinking there
are times when I need you less.

My light is here all the time—even when
I am not—even when I am not aware of it.
God, I'm glad *you're* here always, *especially*
when I am least aware of your nearness.
In the name of Him who said, "I am the Light."

Amen.

Thank Goodness

Lord, I am so very grateful today! I feel
like saying "Yes!" to life! . . . "yes" to its
tensions and its peace . . . "yes" to its
sufferings and its joys . . . "yes" even to
death, for even in death I will not be
separated from you.

Thank you for my "yes." Thank you for your
"Yes!"-to-the-world in Jesus Christ.
Thank you for your "yes" to my humanity, your
"yes" to pain, your "yes" to death . . . and
the Good News of your "Yes!" by overcoming
these!

"Yes!" God . . . thank you *very, very* much.

Amen.

Others Should Be Better Americans

Lord Jesus, I think others should feed the hungry.
Others should clean up the environment.
Others should work in your Church.
Others should stand up for the downtrodden.
Others should witness and tell people about trust in Christ.
Others should give more.

Others should be less prejudiced.
Others should be better Americans.
Others should be better Christians on their jobs.

I'm really concerned, God. Things in this world are in a mess. Others should *do* something about it! They should get up off their rear ends and get to work! Others should fall down on their knees before you.

God, do you understand the problem? . . .

I Can't Shake the Call

"Come with me. I will make you fishers of men."
———Mark 1:17 (Paraphrased)

Lord Jesus, it seems old-fashioned,
fanatical—but I can't shake the call to
follow you. I want to know more about it
before I commit myself. I am afraid to let go
and trust you fully.

Sometimes I think I am a Christian because
I'm active in church and read devotional
messages at work and try to lead a halfway
decent life. But you call me to trust, to obey,
to serve mankind (even here at work).

Give me strength to be a disciple 100% today . . .
and one day at a time.

Amen.

When I Feel Separated

Holy Spirit, I do not want this day to be filled with useless exercises.

I want to feel united with you. I want this day to be perfectly resigned to you.

Today I would renounce everything that separates me from you. Today I would work in an attitude of prayer for those with whom I work.

Holy Spirit, may I do my work for your sake; in Jesus' name.

Amen.

I Hate Hotels and Restaurants

God, thank you for travel. In traveling around
I feel a sense of accomplishment, and I get new
and fresh outlooks.

But I get lonesome. I hate hotels and restaurants
when I am alone. I don't like silence or idleness
without my family near.

I fill these idle hours with entertainment.
My value system is different—I do things I
wouldn't do at home, and then wonder why things
aren't the same when I get home. Forgive me.

God, thank you for travel; for the words,
"I am with you always, even to the end of
the world." . . . and, thank you for home.

Amen.

Thanks a Million

Heavenly Father, thank you for the joys
of living in this country, for the thrill of
competition, for the good rewards . . . for a
challenging job . . . for the loyalty that some
people have . . . for the loyalty that I have
to some people . . . for my competitors, who make
me do a good job . . . for real friends, not just
"associates" . . . for good working conditions . . .
for today's opportunity . . . for coffee and
cokes . . . for the joy of working on a team . . . for
the times that I am aware of others who have
so much less; through Jesus Christ.

Amen.

Hire the Handicapped

The sign on my way to work today said:
"Hire the Handicapped."

Help those who are not free physically—the sick,
those who can't control their muscles, those
who are missing a limb, the sightless who sit in
darkness; the deaf whose every day is silent.

Comfort those who *fear* the loss of health or
dread old age.

Grant a rich *inward* freedom to those who have
so little outward freedom.

And as long as I call you Lord——you who healed
the sick, and fed the hungry, and helped the downtrodden——I must make a response to that sign I
saw on the way to work today . . .

Amen.

Just Getting By

When I act humble enough to hide my pride—
    forgive me.
When I show enough respect so he won't see
    my contempt—forgive me.
When I point to my good work to cover up
    the bad—forgive me.
When I give just enough to hide real
    selfishness—forgive me.
When I talk to cover up my insecurity—
    forgive me.
When I show enough interest to hide my
    lack of love—forgive me.

Now that I've confessed, God, I feel better.
Don't let me stop with prayers that just make
me feel better. God, help me to do something
about them. Please.

                      Amen.

Is That All There Is?

God, my work doesn't always
have meaning. I seem to be a
functionary, carrying out my
function just to exist. Nothing I do seems to give meaning
to my vocation.

Forgive me when I think that
meaning is *automatically* tied
up with my work, and when I
think that meaning in life
comes from *my* efforts . . . and
not from you.

Keep me from trying so
frantically to *make* my work
meaningful: help me to *find* the
meaning that *you* have for me in
my work. Help me to turn over
my feverish ways to you. Grant
that I may say, "Thy will be
done."

*　　*　　*

Thy will be done.

Amen.

Do I Want Too Much Credit?

"Unless the Lord builds the house, those
who build it work in vain. Unless the Lord
watches over the city, the guard stays
awake in vain. It is vain that you get up
early and go to bed late, eating the bread
of anxious toil; for he gives sleep to his
beloved."

——Psalm 127:1–2 (Paraphrased)

*   *   *

God, so many times my way seems better than
yours. I want to be in the center of action,
and get the credit . . . and I end up "eating the
bread of anxious toil."

God, let me build with you; watch with you;
rest with you.

Enter my heart and mind now—during this
moment of quiet.

Let's get to work—*your* way!

Amen.

My Love Runs Out

"Give thanks to the Lord, for his love is
steadfast. Give thanks to the God of gods,
for his steadfast love endures. O give thanks to
the Lord of lords, for his steadfast love
endures forever."

——Psalm 136:1–3 (Paraphrased)

God, your love endures. Mine doesn't.
I'm glad yours outlasts my lack of it.
Thank you, in Jesus' name.

Amen.

You Love the Ones Who Smell Bad

"May the Lord answer you in the day of trouble! May
he send you help from the sanctuary. May he grant
your heart's desire.

——Psalm 20:1–2, 4 (Paraphrased)

God, this is my prayer for the poor; for those who
smell bad; those who are not clean; who speak
poor English.

But for your grace, I would be in their place. . . .
I know you love them as well as you love me. Help me
to love them, too, and help me to show it.
Use *me* as intercessor in my intercessory prayer; for the
sake of Jesus Christ.

Amen.

Show Me How To Love

"Happy is every one who loves the Lord, who walks
in his ways! You shall eat of the fruit of your
labor; you shall be happy, and all shall be well
with you."

——Psalm 128:1–2 (Paraphrased)

God, show me how to love you more—myself less.
Help me to praise you more—myself less.
Help me to love more those who work alongside me—
myself less. Help me to be more aware of them
and their feelings—myself less. Help me to
serve others more—myself less. Help me—
for Jesus' sake.

Amen.

SUMMER

Thanks for Work

God, thank you for my work . . .
for the rewards of hard work . . .
for this country and the prosperity we enjoy . . .
for all whose work benefits me . . .
for teamwork . . .
for the real satisfaction of doing a good job . . .
for a new chance when I have done a poor job . . .
for friendships . . .
for responsibility. . .
for a pleasant place to work . . .
for those who care enough to be honest . . .
and for the Life that was perfectly lived, and was given
for me.

Amen.

When I Am Wrong

God, I confess that I am a sinner.
And I confess that this sounds good but it generally
doesn't mean anything to me.
Help me to be specific:
I confess that I am selfish when I _____

_____

My sin of omission _____
bothers me and I think it bothers you.
My sin of commission _____
is one you would have me stop.
God, when I am truthful my list is long, my need great,
and my strength small.
Forgive my empty words. Help me be specific; in Jesus'
name.

Amen.

When I Doubt

"We are more than conquerors through him who loves us. For neither death
nor life, nor things present nor future things, nor anything else, can separate
us from the love of God in Christ Jesus our Lord."
——Romans 8:37–38 (Paraphrased)

*   *   *

God, here I am again . . .
I do not know who you are . . .
or where you are . . .
or what you are . . .
but I do know *that* you are . . .

I have many doubts. There is part of me that always doubts.
But there is part of me that never doubts, for you have been real to me.
Be near to me today as I begin another day's work; through Christ the risen Lord.

Amen.

Help Me Feel Your Joy

Open my *ears* today to the words you would speak to me through others.

God, open my *mind* to understand truths you would teach me through others.

Open my *heart* to feel your love and joy and acceptance through others.

Open my *mouth* only to truth, love, and thoughtfulness
. . .
that I may give them to you through others.

Open my *hands* to the warmth of touch, the freedom of giving, the joy of hard work . . .
dedicated to you through others.

For the sake of Christ my Lord.

Amen.

Turn the Company Upside Down

God, it's so easy to value someone by what he can
master, and not by what
masters him. Today may I see others as ones you love
just as much as
you love me.

May our organization-chart be turned upside down so
that managers assist
employees to get *their* work done.

May we not see employees as those who work for us—
may we work for them.
May our work together be more meaningful as we help
each other.

May I dare to try the words: "the first shall be last and
the last first";
"Let him who is first be servant of all." Strengthen me
to see that these
words of Jesus apply to my life and my work—today.

Amen.

In the Middle of Nowhere

God, I'm wishy-washy, I can see both sides.

I understand many things a little, but nothing enough
to live by.

Hawks are too vengeful, doves are too naïve.
Activists have lost their faith, pietists their love and
concern.
The young are too brash, the old are too set in their
ways.

Racists and race liberals—both seem to have too much
prejudice (even if it is expressed differently!).

So here I am, God—nowhere!
Nowhere for You! And I *still* don't feel so strongly
about
one way that I can give it my all.

God, I don't even know whether to ask for forgiveness
or guts, love or
reconciliation.

Just grant me what *you* know I need.

Amen.

Let Freedom Ring

God, *I pray for my country.* From every mountainside, let freedom ring.

May my country be, to your glory, a sweet land of liberty. May her

citizens *never* say "My country, right or wrong!" but may we

determine to work that our nation's policy be consistent with

Jesus Christ. Grant her citizens (starting with me) a new patriotism—

to defend her when she is right, to protest where she is wrong. And

the humble wisdom to discern between the two.

I *pray for my company.* May it be "people-conscious."

May "corporate" mean "community"; "profit" mean "fulfillment for all."

May "loyalty" mean "both ways," and "policy" mean "common good" . . .

all that we might glorify you, as a country . . . as a company.

Amen.

Please Don't Fold, Bend, or Staple
Depersonalization

God, sometime I feel like a card with one corner
clipped off.
Please don't fold, bend, staple, or deface me.

Punch my holes in the right columns so the sorter will
put me in
the right stack. And please don't mix the cards in my
stack
by color!

Help me get to the top of the stack. Keep me active—I
dread
being stored away in those cardboard boxes.

        *   *   *

God, I'm glad I can smile when I pray. And, I'm glad
that I'm
not really No. 9805426 to you.

                              Amen.

When You Said Yes

God, once I answered "yes" to you. I felt good about it, but here at work I'm not sure what this "yes" means.

But I *do* know one *attitude* I could change: _____
_____

I do know one *ambition* I should change: _____
_____

God, maybe there *is* a "handle" to what it means to say "yes" to you.
And, thank you for saying "yes" to me; in Jesus Christ.

Amen.

I Put Off Getting Started

God, I'm afraid of failing. I don't like to begin a job, for
it will be
judged. Tension comes in thinking "Will it be good
work?" for I, too,
will be judged.

I put off getting started. I procrastinate. I do all the
little things first, to keep from turning to my big task: I
clean up, I get ready. God, I hate to get started!

In prayer, you seem to understand. Thanks. You don't
give me any clichés to manipulate me.

Jesus entered into my condition when he said, "Let this
cup pass from me." Thank you, God.

Amen.

When I Feel Locked In

Jesus, you had no place to lay your head. I do.

There is much that is appealing about your life on
earth—
you were free to move around. I'm not; that's why I
feel
locked in.

Locked in by my mortgage, my job, my pension,
my seniority. What looked like security is
really inflexibility.

If I felt free, the locks would be gone.
Then I would be free to *choose* to stay here in my job.

Jesus, grant me some of the freedom you showed.

Amen.

Why Me?

Why did you choose *me*, God? I'm no stronger than anyone else here. My faith isn't pure.

Why did you choose *this job*, God? Most of the time I don't even think of having a vocation to this kind of work.

Why did you choose *these* people, God, for me to be around? There are lots of places I'd rather be.

Why did you choose me, God, to be your man, in this work, among these people?

Why did I choose today, God, to ask the question? Perhaps I'm ready for your answer. Lead me.

Amen.

Janitor to President

Jesus, you taught us to pray *"Our* Father," not "my Father."
Thank you for the feeling of community as we begin this day's
work. *Our* Father, means the Father of all of us: janitor to president, trainee to chairman.

God, we can know you as *Our* Father only if we are brothers.
Make me a bridge-builder over gaps: the color gap, the experience gap, the emotional gap; that we might
be a group whose work together declares "Our Father
. . ."

Amen.

Profit, Income, and Dividends

"Give us this day our daily bread." Lord, you taught us to pray
for daily bread—but instead we pray for life overflowing with
conveniences, for affluence-that-shows. Our anxiety concerns
profit, income, pension, advancement, dividends.

I guess we take daily bread for granted . . . maybe that's
where we miss the boat. Jesus said to pray for the
essentials—for daily bread. We pray for the
nonessentials, even the excesses.

God, teach us again about the simplicity of a well-ordered
life. Forgive the web of nonessentials that we weave;
through Christ our Lord.

Amen.

Yes-men and Apple Polishers

"Forgive us our sins as we forgive those who sin against us."
God, we need your help even to get through this part.
Forgive us when we *withhold* forgiveness!

Forgive us our sins: for allowing suspicion to come between us, for being yes-men and apple-polishers, or for hating yes-men and apple-polishers who may get ahead.

Forgive us our sins: for not making our instructions clear, and driving others with guilt; for giving someone responsibility without authority.

Forgive us our sins: for taking credit and giving little, for rarely saying "thank you," "nice job."

Forgive us our sins as we forgive those who sin against us.

Amen.

First Things First

God, as I begin this day, fill my soul with the beauty of harmony with you. Grant me continual refreshment in union
with you.

Grant me rest in my labor, a sense of humor when I take
life too seriously; peace, when life is too congested. Keep the eyes of my heart uplifted. Help me feel the beauty of colors, of sparkling sounds, of a mind stayed on you.

Grant me today the inexpressible joy of a day spent consciously in your presence, the joy of a will yielded to yours; in Jesus' name.

Amen.

Could This Be Me?

God, grant that today I
may be a little

    quieter . . .

        more gentle . . .

    more loving . . .

        fairer . . .

    more honest . . .

        more myself.

    . . . for Christ's sake.

            Amen.

I Work Here

God, this is where I work. I'm back for another day.
It is comfortable here. I fit. Thank you. These
walls separate me from millions of others whose work is
different.

I spend a lot of time in this room. I have had
joys and sorrow, rewards and disappointments, here.
Some of what I do is routine . . . some is exciting.
I've done things here I'm proud of; and done
things here I'm ashamed of. In a real sense
this place is a part of me.

I'm glad you know about the place where I
work. I'm glad you're here.

Amen.

Be Seated

God, this is my chair. It faces my work. I spend
a lot of time in it.

My *faith* is like this chair. I rest in it,
and it confronts my vocation. May my faith in
you never be turned around backward—away from my
work—separated.

May my faith flow into all my work; through
Jesus Christ.

Amen.

Dial Tone

God, this is my telephone. It is an opportunity and sometimes a problem.

I can reach others with it.

I, too, can be used to reach others for you.

Just as this phone is linked with others by an unending system of wires, help me to see that I, too, am linked with others in you; through your unending grace.

Amen.

Credit Cards, Pictures, and Money

God, this is my wallet. It tells a great deal
about me——pictures, credit cards, money,
membership
cards; and it "fits" my pocket. I don't know it's
there!

Thank you for pictures of loved ones. Thank you for
my country whose money says, "In God We Trust."
Thank you for credit cards, and for trust and
honesty upon which our economy is built.

God, your blessings "fit"—I forget about
them and take them for granted. Thank you
for not forgetting me.

Amen.

Future Shock

God, this is my calendar. Summer is passing by.
It looks so "orderly"—each day looks the same.
Each week looks so even.

My week is *not* orderly, and is anything *but* a
straight line. I don't even know what today will hold!

But you know what is in store for me in the future—
you know which month will be my last.

Thank you for your majesty and providence, even if
it does remind me of how little I really do control.
I am glad that you are God of all the weeks and
all the months. Use me in *your* way in each of
these days.

Amen.

Life on the Go

Dear God, so often I am afraid of time. I am uncomfortable
if I am not busy. Show me when running is a retreat
into "busyness."

Forgive me for wanting feverish activity—I don't
really plan it that way. I like to think of myself as a
"man on the go." Help me to consider "life on the go—
to where?"; life on the go—*how?*"; "life on the go—
for whom?"

Help me to "be still and know that you are God." I do
not pray for laziness, but for help to see myself just
as I really am.

Your peace passes my understanding—help me to
understand more about the quiet and order of the
days spent in your will.

Amen.

When I Go Home Alone

God, I work with others all day long. We are like
sardines—

and all moving! But at the end of the day I go home
alone—

all alone. I go to another world—of family and home,
where there is love and sometimes pain, and joy, and
too many

evenings out. I am *more* than just a working person—
for

I am a playing, sleeping, family person.

Others with whom I work also have private lives. I
don't

often think about this. I don't know their families. I
don't *really* know my fellow workers—not in their
personal loves and hopes and pains.

God, forgive me for seeing others only as "workday"
people.
Strengthen us in *all* of life.

Amen.

You're the Boss

God, my Employer, who hires without discrimination,
who *gives* all that you require, who fires none;
God, whose Personnel Department is universal, whose
retirement plan is eternal, I have a major concern
now:

" _____

_____

_____ . "

What is your answer, and your concern for me?"

_____

_____

Live It to the Hilt

Father, may I not ask "What *must* I do?", but learn to ask,
"What *may* I do?" May I grasp the opportunity of this day,
and live it to the hilt with you.

Make today important to me. Yesterday is just a memory—tomorrow is just a vision and a plan.
I cannot live in them today—not even when I want to.

God, it is so much easier to face yesterday or tomorrow!
Walk with me today, and help me to live just one day at a time.

Amen.

I Don't Want to Hurt

God, why don't I suffer because of my faith?
If I were perfectly Christian would I be rejected
by the world and crucified? Sometimes it worries
me that I don't suffer.

I don't *want* to suffer—I don't even like to
bring it up! But it bothers me. What would
happen to me if I stood up for justice right here
at work? God, I want to deserve your love. Does
suffering earn it?

But grant me freedom from trying to deserve or
earn your love. Deliver me from a martyr complex.
And because you *do* love me, may I stand for the
gospel whatever suffering may come. I ask this in
the name of Him who suffered for me.

Amen.

FALL

Labor Day

God, I pray for those whose possibility of success is
limited by education,
color, or environment. Direct those whose work is dull
and uncreative,
and unrewarded. . . . Comfort those who are not able
to work—the
physically and mentally handicapped; the old, and those
looking for work. . . .
I pray for those whose work is paralyzed by fear or
guilt or family
pressure.

I pray for those whose work is simply for themselves—
where tensions
are high and rewards are empty. . . . God, grant me
joyous spontaneity of
work done in your care. May my work express my faith
in Jesus as Lord of Life.

Amen.

A Name or a Number?

God, I feel like a number. Sometimes I get treated like a quantity.

My work is used like an "ingredient" or a "part" that's replaceable.

God, I don't like the subtle pressures that control so much of me.

But I confess that I use others, too. I treat them like functionaries and job descriptions. How do I do otherwise? Please
show me.

Show me today, God, what it means to "do unto others as I would
have them do unto me." Show me, please—give me an illustration. *Make* me an illustration; for Jesus Christ's sake.

Amen.

I'm Grateful

God, thank you for the feeling I have at seeing a friend when I am
in a strange place and alone . . . for new acquaintances, and the
first time that someone calls me by name.

Thank you for the few people to whom I can say, "I am lonesome"—and
who don't just try to change my mind or cheer me up!

Thank you for the times when I bear another's pain—
the few times that I don't have to cover up the pain of quiet with empty words.

Thank you for the times when I know that *you are God;*
and when I listen as well as speak.

Amen.

Give Me Security

Almighty and eternal God, I
give myself to you for the
living of today.

Take my ambitions and give
me your goals. Take my fears
and give me your calm. Take
the security that comes from
"getting" and give me the
security that comes in giving.

Amen.

When I Feel Guilty

"If we say we don't sin, we fool ourselves and the truth is not
in us. If we confess our sins, God is faithful and just, and will forgive our unrighteousness."

—— I John 1:8-9 (Paraphrased).

God, it is humbling to accept your forgiveness rather than
holding on to my guilt. It is hard to admit that there is nothing I can do about guilt. I guess that's what repentance is.

God, I feel *sorry* about some things, but help me truly to
repent and turn over my day to you; through Christ my Lord.

Amen.

For My Wife's Touch

God, thank you for my wife—for being able to share joys
and sorrows, setbacks and accomplishments. Thank you for her
understanding, for her touch, for her love, and for her respect in spite of my faults.

Thank you for her encouragement when I am down, and for
putting up with me when I am up. May I be as interested,
as thoughtful, and as understanding of her.

God, grant that we may not glibly pretend our marriage
is perfect—may we always be able to talk things over, and be really honest with each other. Help each of us to listen . . . and to listen as *you* would speak to us; through Jesus Christ our Lord.

Amen.

Thank You for Home

God, thank you for home; for a place to go when I am tired and

weary. Make it a place to take troubles—not a place where

troubles grow. Make it a place to take fears—not a place

to learn fear and mistrust. . . .

. . . A place to take the disappointments—not a place to cause disappointments . . . a place to take rejections—not a

place to be rejected . . . a place to take loneliness—not a place to be made lonely.

May our home send forth love, in Christ's name.

Amen.

Colleagues, Clients, and a Cup

God, why did you tell me to love others, to treat all men
as brothers? I have tried—my colleagues, my clients,
the needy, the hurting—I have tried, but I come to you
disillusioned.

God, it was so peaceful—the status quo. "Our way of life"
was so comfortable. I was cozy and contented.

And when I tried to love others, I hurt too much. I
don't like to see pain or hear problems. It's too much
sometimes, Father, let this cup pass from me. . . .

. . . nevertheless, your will, not mine, be done. Into
your hands I commit my spirit.

Amen.

When I Take My Work Too Seriously

God, I'm glad you have a sense of humor! I wish the Pharisees could have laughed at themselves!

I think the home in Nazareth was alive with fun; and the
fraternity of twelve apostles must have laughed and sang.

God, when I take my work so seriously help me to be able to
laugh at myself.

Amen.

Do I Dare Pray?

O God, my heavenly Father,
my heart soars to be perfectly
rested in you, perfectly guided
by you, perfectly serving you,
perfectly yielded to your will.

Dare I to pray that you do
with me what you please? I
want to—what an adventure that
would be!

May today be lived in no
other motive but love of you,
and willingness to be forgiven
when I fail. You are the
potter, I am the clay. I pray
for a day of continual
communion with you.

Today may I live in confi-
dence in you, with love and
humility; through Jesus
Christ my Lord.

Amen.

Thank God It's Friday!

God, here I am at work again. I'm glad the week is
almost over . . .
but some people don't have jobs today.

Guide and comfort those who have lost their jobs,
in their time of worry and self-distrust.

To those who are retiring, grant patience through their
times of loneliness and the fear of stagnation.

I pray for those who cannot work because of a
handicap of health or human injustice; and for those
whose work
is dull and unnoticed.

Thank you for the vocation of this work you have given
me. Lead me, Lord.

Amen.

My Office Door Is Open

It opens to the private lives of others; it closes to give me privacy—thank you for quiet and time alone.

I pass through this door at the most important times of the day—
the beginning and the end. What I accomplish during the day
depends, in part, on my outlook when I come in; and what has
been done shows on my face when I leave.

Grant that I may deny myself and follow you today. After
work is done for today, may I close this door on a day
spent with the knowledge of your presence . . . in the name of
Him who said, "I am the Way"; "Behold, I stand at the door
and knock."

Amen.

Looking Out the Office Window

I have this view all year around.

But this window shows me the *variety* in your
creation and care—rain and light, snow
and sun, the changing colors of each season,
and different sounds. . . .

And I see from this window man's use of
beauty and life.

I can see my neighbors—your children—
all sorts of people, in their joys and needs, in
their loves and fears.

May the windows of my life be clean so that I
can always see, and *be*, a neighbor. God, help
me so that I will not *just* stop and stare out of
my window; in Jesus' name.

Amen.

Succeeding in Business

God, I'm afraid of failing. I would like to rise to the
top.
I want to be big in the children's eyes. I want my wife
to
be proud of me.

I guess these are okay to want, but they make pressure
on me.

Sometimes the pressure is so great that I try to be
someone I'm not. I try to look important. I try to
act important. I try to dominate.

I want success, but God, I don't trust it either—
I've seen what success does to some people. I
want real success and real humility—
lots of both of them! But I know I don't get
either by just wanting them.

May I simply strive to live for you and to please
you only.

Amen.

My Name on the Door

It is nice for others to know who I am—
to call me by name. Thank you for revealing
yourself and inviting me to call *you* by name.

My nameplate is personal—it is mine. It tells
others that what is done here is my creation
and accomplishment . . . and it reminds me that
I am *responsible* for what is done here.

Thank you for my name. I give it to my children,
just as you have given us yours. We are
Christians. Thank you! In your name
we pray.

Amen.

Push-and-Pull

God, in the push-and-pull of this morning's work, lift my eyes to look at the future.

I become what I do. I belong to whatever has my allegiance. I am shaped by my associations. I become what I long for . . . what I plan . . . what I pray.

But, most of all, I become what I *do*.

May I do what *you* want by responding to the demands of Christ. Bring me to his judgment, his forgiveness, his freedom.

God, in this hurried world of hard work and little planning, help my "becoming."

Amen.

Generally Speaking

God, I don't like it when you get specific . . .
I like the words, "The first shall be last";
but I don't want to be last.

I want to be forgiven in general, but it's
hard to accept forgiveness for my selfish
ambitions and my overindulgence.

I want to enjoy freedom in general; but not
freedom from my prejudice, or from my hurting
others to get ahead.

I know that I should love my neighbor and my enemy
in general; but I don't like it when this means
to love the company politician, my next-door
neighbor, or the Chinese.

God, help me to pray, "Thy *specific* will be done,"
in my life.

Amen.

All Things to All People

"Do I seek the favor of men, or of God?
Am I trying to please men or God? If I
were still pleasing men, I should not be
a servant of Christ."

——Gal. 1:10 (Paraphrased)

*   *   *

God, I see committed men all around me;
men working hard, sacrificially, long hours,
taking home the worries. I do, too.

But in the great hurry of business, I don't
see commitment to you. I don't see "freedom"
or "simplicity". . . .

Perhaps I'm looking in the wrong way. It
would be easy to put my whole trust in Christ
if others just would . . . but he didn't say it
would be easy.

God, I want to be willing—*completely* willing—
to follow you today.

Amen.

When the Spark Dies

Lord, time spent consciously with you is so very good.
It is not describable in words. In your presence there
is the joy of expanded vision, the feeling of wonder
and power and life and recreation.

I seem to know myself, to have new insights. I know
more of life—and more *about* life.

But it fades—my awareness of you. It goes
quietly and surely, even when I would hang on
to it.

Thank you, God, for giving so much of yourself.
Thank you for the faith that knows you are
here even when I forget . . . help my unbelief.

Amen.

I Don't Care

God, help me to show to others today the kindness
I crave from them. It is easy in my work to
miss the cry of suffering, to put patriotism
above allegiance to you, to assume that minority
persons have full freedom.

I pray for the men of my company. Help them
in the pressures that they live with—creative
pressures; destructive pressures.

I pray for the women who work here—whose
lives are divided between home and office;
children and bosses.

Strengthen our cares and concerns for
each other; in Christ's name.

Amen.

When I'm Mad

God, you know my heart much better than I do.
Much of the time I am hostile. It comes out
as I try to change others, when I try to
prove that I'm always right, when I get tied
up in knots trying to speak in a group.

My hostility is sometimes focused on others—
the church, the government, the company.

Forgive me for hating my frailties so
much.

Amen.

Religion Is Good Business

God, a little bit of Christianity makes good business
Church activities look good on my résumé . . .
being a friend is good business . . . to lead a
moral life makes for respect.

I am a friend to the friendly—make me a friend
to the friendless. I accept the part of
religion that helps me in my work—
help me to go deeper, and learn sacrifice
and discipleship.

God, save me from religion that is just good
business. Teach me the example of Him who
lived as a Suffering Servant . . . for me; in His name.

Amen.

When I Want To Get Away

God, how nice it would be to get away . . .
to leave behind the clock, the datebook, the revolving
door . . . and the treadmill. I just want to rest; to be
free from responsibility.

Yet without these things I wouldn't be happy either.
. . .

So the freedom I really want is not freedom *from*
responsibility; it is freedom *within* responsibility.
I need the assurance that you are with me.

God, grant meaning in the hurried pace of my work.
Grant me freedom from living in doubt and fear and
mistrust. Grant me the joy of freedom *for*
responsibility, freedom *for* others,
freedom *for you;* in Jesus' name.

Amen.

God Bless America

Veterans' Day reminds me more of parades
than of those who gave their lives to win
freedom. Save me from treating so lightly
the rich heritage that is your gift to this
country.

Thank you for making me an American. May
it not be old-fashioned to be thrilled by
the Stars and Stripes or the National
Anthem. I love my country. May I love
her enough to stand up for loyalty and patriotism;
and love her enough to protest and make my voice
heard when she requires things against my
Christian conscience. . . . Thank you for the
lives of those who would make America free and
just. God *bless* America.

                                        Amen.

My Family

Father, I pray for my family. Sometimes there is
tension; sometimes disappointment; sometimes I
get mad. A few times I have a *right* to be;
many times I don't.

Give us an understanding of each other. The children
are in school now—bless them in the tensions
and problems they face. Don't let me forget
that they have competition as much as I do.
May our love grow.

At home, work is being done—cleaning,
planning, chauffeuring—maybe dull, thankless
work. May I change that by understanding and
an occasional "Thank you, darling."

Thank you, God, for my family.

Amen.

When I Gripe a Lot

God, forgive my griping. I don't want to be a negative person—I really don't. But many times I am swept along in grumbling about anything and everything.

I know that being negative toward "them" and toward life is a sign of dissatisfaction with myself.
I *am* dissatisfied with me—you must be, too.

What's wrong, God? Is it you? Is it life?
Is it others? Is it I?

Amen.

People Are the Most Important Things

Dear Lord, who shows compassion and interest
in all who need it; I don't. When someone
gets back to work after a tragedy or suffering,
it's easy to say "Welcome back!" but it's hard for me
to take the time to feel *with* a person how it
really hurts, how it's hard to start back to
work again.

Increase in me the realization that people are
the most important things here—people whose
lives can be free in Christ.

Help my listening. Help my caring. And God,
grant me an ear that's attached to my heart,
and a faith that's attached to my feet;
in Jesus' name.

Amen.

I'm Not Getting Any Younger

God, I am not getting any
younger. I feel empty when I
think of others who have passed
me by, or might pass me by.
Sometimes others seem to have
everything going their way. If
I only had another chance!
Things might turn out differently!

But God, they might *not* turn
out differently. I guess
things could be a great deal
worse. . . . I have limitations.
Show them to me and help me to
accept them. This is so hard.
Show me what purpose you have
for me today to use to the *very
fullest* the gifts that I do
have.

Amen.

Driving Home from Work

God, I'm driving home from
work. Kids are standing in the
street. Will that boy
learn to be a man? Who will
teach him?

Why does that boy have it so
rough and I have it so good?
Who will give him the ambition
I have, the opportunity I had?

God, will his ambition be
turned to bitterness? Will his
boldness turn to servility to
survive? Or will it turn to
rebellion when survival doesn't
matter?

Will he hear my prayers for
brotherhood even though I don't
pray with him? Will he know
I've changed and I'm thinking
about him?

What kind of a man will he be?

Lord, what kind of a man am I?

Amen.

Rush Rush Rush

God, can you be in all the rush I see? Whistles blow
and people punch clocks. Lights change and impatience
pushes through traffic . . . where are you among the
commercials, interruptions, revolving doors, signs?
among the elevator buttons, steno pools, telephones,
salesmen, machinery?

Lord, take hold of me. In the pressures of work
I see with blinders. I miss the beauty, the
simplicity. Lift my eyes to the hills, my
thoughts to the mind of Christ, my ears to
stillness.

Thank you, God. In you is wholeness. Forgive
my feverish seeking. Make *me* to be more
easily found in the rush.

Amen.

Did I Pass on the Other Side?

God, thank you for sleep . . . for clean sheets . . .
for being waked up by someone I love . . . for
coffee . . .
for my warm coat . . . for my car. Thank you for
heaters . . . and street cleaners . . . and for the
person who let me in line. Thank you for the
janitor . . . the U.S. mail . . . for telephone operators.
Thank you for work . . . and breaks from it . . . and
jokes . . .
and pleasant waitresses.

Thank you for quitting time . . . and the good
feeling of locking up for the day . . . for policemen . . .
and newsboys . . . for music on my radio. God, did I
pass by a person today who doesn't have these things?
Did I pass by on the other side? Forgive me. Give
me vision beyond my sight. Make me a neighbor
beyond my neighborhood.

Amen.

I Get Paid Today

God, it's the end of another month. I get my
check today. It just shows dollars and cents.
It won't show the sweat, the tense times, the
frustrations; or the love and fulfillment
that made up the month.

My work is valued in quantities . . . and I like money.
Thank you for giving me life and work and
everything I need to earn it. And thank you
for the privilege of stewardship.

But I am glad life is not *all* dollars and cents.
When I take this check home, may I take home not just
a quantity, but a great deal more—my love, my
time, my interest; in Jesus' name.

Amen.

WINTER

When Someone Needs Me

If I were not a Christian
today would I act differently?
Because of my trust in Christ
will I be more understanding
today? Will I love more, be
more helpful, more relaxed,
more hopeful, more joyous?

God, there is probably
someone I know, who needs to be
helped . . . to be understood.
May I be in no hurry. May I
think of his need as I visit or
telephone him.

God, plant in me today the
words, "Inasmuch as you have
done it unto the least of one
of these my brethren, you have
done it unto me."

Amen.

I'm the Boss

God, I don't like to correct someone. I like
to encourage and reward, but not correct.
It's hard to point out errors without feeling like
a pushover or a god.

But work has got to be done correctly—
others' jobs depend on it, too.

God, I wish I had some laws to go by or some
direct word from you as to what to do in every
situation.

When I have to discipline someone or say no,
give me fair judgment—and may I act in love;
in Jesus' name.

Amen.

Things Are in a Mess

Come, Lord Jesus! *to our world.*
Danger's rampant and poverty is spreading.
The sick of many lands go unattended—
death and sorrow deal a heavy hand. War
continues while many cry for peace . . . Come,
Lord Jesus . . .

Come, Lord Jesus! *to our family.*
Television blasts our time together into
divided worlds. Demands of school and
work pull us apart. Prayer's a farce
when we're together. Come, Lord Jesus . . .

Come, Lord Jesus! *to my heart.*
I ask for goodness—I beg for light . . .
but I do not live by the light I already know.

Come, Lord Jesus!

Amen.

Prayer for My Family

God, by birth we are a family. By custom
we sit down to eat together. By habit we
pray together or we do not pray together.
Grant us a closer relationship than biology
and custom and habit.

Help us to share each other's disappointments.

Help us to feel that we have a shoulder to cry on
when we are scared.

Help us to feel loved enough that we don't
have to keep our problems inside of us.

Help us to feel the forgiveness offered through
trust in Christ.

Draw us closer to each other, closer to
you, closer to our brothers in the world . . .
as he was.

Amen.

When We Sit Around the Table

God, how good it is that we are together!
Sometimes we feel cut off from each other.
Forgive our separate search for happiness
and meaning, when they are as near to us as breath.
We look in high places, in feverish activity—
we *over*look a simple manger, a simple night,
and Christ in all of us who sit around this table.

God, make me conscious of the pressures of schoolwork,
of housework. Make them conscious of the pressures
of my work; that we all might appreciate and
understand each other.

Be our unseen Guest, that our lives together might
be graceful, and thankful, and sacrificial.

Amen.

Christmas Eve with the Family

God, we thank you for Christmas Eve! It doesn't seem like another whole year is past! We remember last year's joy in the children's faces as the lights of the tree sparkled in their eyes. We remember happy times together. Thank you for memories. Even the sad times have made our love grow for you and for each other.

God, we're glad for the occasion to give gifts to each other!

We included so much love—so much of ourselves, as we wrapped the packages that are under the tree. Thank you for the joys of giving. Thank you for tears of joy.

Thank you for the birth of Jesus, the Christ, our Lord.

Amen.

Christmas Hugs in Bathrobes

God, what a wonderful day! The joys of
children in wishes-come-true. The wonder
and amazement of Santa Claus that teaches us
so much about gifts undeserved, about
mystery and wonder, about love and joy.

Thank you for the warm hugs of our family in
bathrobes as we unwrapped gifts—these are
touches of love that will warm our souls forever.

Happy birthday, Jesus! Be born in our hearts
and our home this day. We feel your nearness
today especially—we feel warm, and loved,
and full. Stay in our home and in our lives.
We know you will as we make a place for you.
Thank you for living, and for dying, and for
rising, and for living with us.

Amen.

Christmas Holidays

God, thank you for good food, for the joys of Christmas,
for the phone call. We pray for
those who did not have a happy Christmas—for those
who
are far from loved ones, for those who
are sick, or hurt, or the brunt of prejudice.
For those who were disappointed, those who did
not receive at Christmas, and those who did not
(or could not) give, we pray.

We know some of these people, Father. Strengthen
us as a family to go out and do what we can for
them and for you.

Overcome our embarrassment and our self-
consciousness as we pray together and talk
together about you; worship together and
serve together; in Jesus' name.

Amen.

Family Prayer

O Christ, help us this year to keep Christmas in the
right way
——by forgetting what we have done for others; and
remembering
what they have done for us.

——by tearing down walls of prejudice; and
building up mansions of good will.

——by ceasing to be gloomy about the world situation;
and beginning to work for harmony and neighborliness
in our own community.

——by ceasing to talk so much about the religion of
Jesus; and beginning, in the spirit of Christmas,
to live it.

——by ceasing to trust in our own goodness; and
beginning to
trust wholly in Christ.

——by ceasing to wallow in guilt; and beginning more
completely to accept his forgiveness.

Amen.

Thank You for Bowl Games

Lord Jesus, thank you for football, for bowl games
and TV, for basketball, for snow, and for time off.

Thank you for the food that sustains us, for antacid
medicine,
for new clothes we have, and for the special
unexpected
gift!

Thank you for crisp winter air, for the warmth of our
home, and for children outside with shiny new bicycles
and wagons and skates.

Thank you for the kind word that someone said to us,
and the someone who appreciated us.

Thank you for the roof that shelters, and for
our table and food made ready by loving hands.

Thank you for tranquil moments, graceful days, and for
life.

Thank you, Lord.

Amen.

When I Feel Loved

God, thank you for love that others have for me.
When I am sick and feel guilty about not going
to work, it is good to call in and have others
understand and show their concern. My guilt
vanishes, and all is well again.

Help me to be willing for others to do things for me.
This is not easy—it is embarrassing. God,
grant me the humility to be able to receive as
well as to give, to receive *your* love and gift,
to let Jesus wash my feet.

And God, I'm glad that *you* will receive my
worship and poor prayers.

Amen.

When Life Seems Unfair

Deliver me, my God, from the feeling that life
is unfair to me. Forgive me when I am bitter
because I won't advance as far as I'd dreamed.
Help me to face my limitations without jealousy
of those more gifted than I.

God, I'm glad you don't measure success as I
often do. Give me the joy of using what
talents I have to the best of my ability, leaving all to
you; through Jesus Christ my Lord.

Amen.

Shined Shoes and Polished Images

Forgive me when I think only of shined shoes,
and not of those who shine shoes—when I think
more of style than of people.

May my feet take me to places where I may serve,
but only after they have stood at the foot of
the Cross. May they be found today by the side
of one whose work is not going well—not that
I may focus on the poor work but on the person
and on understanding the "why."

May my feet be faithful, as the Feet that climbed
the stairs to the Upper Room. May they be spent
following in His steps.

Amen.

Use My Hands

Make them productive, like the sweaty, dusty
hands of the Carpenter. Put them to work
serving others, like the Hands that washed the feet
of the disciples. Make them to show love, like the
Hands that healed with a touch.

Make them to do brave things, like the Hands
folded calmly before Pilate. Make them to do
works of witness, like the Hands that broke
Bread and poured Wine. Make them to bear
suffering in your name, like the nail-pierced
Hands.

Use them to call others to you—
hands outstretched in love for all kinds and sorts
and colors of men, like the Hands that beckoned
"Follow Me." Use my hands for him.

Amen.

When I Daydream

God, help me to see things as they really are.
In business it seems like everyone is trying to
influence everyone else. It is hard to see
objectively—to make clear decisions.

Something keeps nagging at me when decisions have
to be made. I guess it's fear of being wrong, and
fear that other people will know it . . . and yet, I *want*
responsibility.

It is not that my task is too hard, but my faith
is too small. Help me to grow; in Jesus' name.

Amen.

I Live By Appointments

God, I live by appointments, by the clock. I go
from meeting to deadline; from report to project.
I know the tensions of competition, of popularity,
of "the company." Forgive my feverish ways.

I do not ask for a lighter load or less work;
but only to have assurance that you are with me, to
give
meaning to my work.

Amen.

Under New Management

God, sometimes all my days seem alike. I fight
the same traffic; I go through the same routine;
I eat in the same places. I feel like saying,
"Color me gray," and I'm scared I'll be doing the
same thing ten years from now!

Show me meaning in my vocation. Grant somehow
that I may see my work today, *all* day, as
completely controlled and ordered by you. You
take over—I'll be "under new management."

O God, help me to *mean* these words as I pray
them; in Jesus' name.

Amen.

The Big Sell and the Glad Hand

God, in this image-conscious world, what do I
look like? Help me to be honest with myself
and with you in this quiet moment.

In the world of the Big Sell, the Glad Hand,
the Smiling Face that hides belligerence—
the world of the clean-cut, the nifty dress, the
arrogance of success, the vanity of refinement,
the haughtiness of social custom . . . in *this*
kind of world I stop long enough to measure
where I fit in, what I look like.

God, help me to be honest with myself and with you
in my silent prayer. . . .

Amen.

Serious Questions Make Me Squirm

*Do I enjoy my work here? Is it satisfying and
fulfilling?*
God, serious questions make me squirm. Help me to
answer honestly
and to know why.
God, do you want me to be here?

What do I want in life? What goals do I have?
God, it is painful to try to find meaning and direction
in life. Help
that my goals will be high ones but realistic.
God, what do *you* want me to do in life? What goals do
you have for me?

Amen.

Self-Examination

Do I criticize others and remain blind to my own limitations?
God, help me to criticize but
only in honesty and in love. May I be big enough to accept others' criticisms of me. Help us to grow.

Do I bring out the best in other people?
God, help me not to dangle before others only
the rewards of money and praise, but may I *share*
the satisfaction of good work, and fulfilling
service; in the name of Jesus Christ.

Amen.

Looking in the Mirror

Am I sensitive to the needs of others where I work?
God, may my own needs not blind me to other people.
Help me to live my Christian faith here in my work.

Do I still kiss my wife? How? When?
God, I am a provider. At home, make me a helper,
a lover, an understander. Help me to live my
Christian faith at home—to be spontaneous in
showing love to my wife and family. And God,
I pray for those husbands and wives who don't
kiss each other anymore.

Amen.

When I Feel Important

God, sometimes I feel like doing you a favor—
like "applying a little Christianity on the job,"
or like asking you to "be with me" at work.

But the process gets reversed. Questions rebound.
My question changes.

Who am I to invite *you* into *my* day?

I can merely turn myself over to you today.

Thank you for taking me into your freedom.

Amen.

Trucks, Tools, and Typewriters

God and Father of this exciting world, you have
opened my eyes to another day. You brightened
the sky, stirring another day. You opened the
gates and doors this morning, garages and
elevators, truck doors and tool boxes.

Motors start, briefcases open to another day,
coffee perks, telephones dial, typewriters
hum, glances exchange, the mail is here.

God, what a wonderful world you made!
It is wonderful not to feel alone today!
Thank you.

Amen.

When I Lose Confidence

Lord, sometimes I seem out of step with you.
Something seems to stand between us—what
is it?

Is it my ambition? Is it my children?
Is it my fear of growing older and being less
productive and being sick? Is it my fear
of failure?

Is it my bitterness, my disappointment,
my hostility, that stands like a black fog
between us?

Is it my looks? my pride? my "style"? that
makes life-in-you less genuine? Is it
my possessions? my righteousness? my "niceness"?

God, don't let me go till I make answer to you.
It won't be easy—I need your help.

Amen.

When I Don't Feel Needed

God, sometimes I feel like I'm not really needed.
Others could get along without me. I spend so
much of my time keeping things stirred up, so
people will notice me. I see everyone else doing the
same thing—so I have to make a place for myself.

What place do *you* have for me today? Lead me in the
order and peace of your way today;
in Jesus' name.

Amen.

Living for Today

God, grant that I may not live in the future.
May the goals I want to reach, and the success
I want to obtain, not rob me of today.

May my future with the company not rob me of
the opportunity of *today* with the company.

Later, when today is just a memory and my
fellow workers are just pictures in an album,
may I know that we were closer to each other
because we were closer to you—every day.

Grant me the joyous spontaneity
of close fellowship with you; through
Jesus Christ my Lord.

Amen.

Look Out for Number One

God, when I am critical, forgive me for saying
"they" instead of "us"; when I praise, forgive
me for saying "I" instead of "we."

When I "look out for Number One!"—I mean *me*
(as if you didn't know). *I* am Number One—
others are secondary—you are secondary
or not even considered. God, forgive me.

But I'm glad I don't have to *win* your favor.
I'm glad I can live in your forgiveness instead
of trying to create my own worth.

And forgive me when I do not live as
one forgiven.

Amen.

Who Am I?

Lord, who am I? Even when I have insights
there seems little satisfaction in knowing.

Much of the time I do what I want. I have it my
way, but there's no freedom in it. I feel like
a hypocrite.

Help me to let you be yourself in life so I can
be myself. Help me feel a unity in myself—
break down the interior partitions between my several
personalities. Flood me with a sense
of fellowship with you because my life is whole
. . . wholly yours; and my vocation is my
ministry; in Jesus' name.

Amen.

One Big Family

God, the Giver of all, if a child of mine
were hungry, even if it were his own fault, I
would do something about it. May I have the
same sensitivity today for the hungry who are
not my children, but who are *your* children, and
my brothers.

God of peace, if my children were fighting, regardless
of the right or wrong, I would try to get them to stop.
May I have courage to do the same when others
at work are involved, or countries in the world are
involved. For all are *your* children.

God of Love, if my children needed to talk with me,
I would listen. Help that I may listen to the
feelings of the lonely. May I be open in honesty
and love, for they are *your* children.

Amen.

When I Feel Like Praying

God, it is good to "feel" like praying; but
it is often for the wrong reasons. Sometimes
I lose myself in the security of reverence and
forget the people outside whom you love.

Often when I withdraw, it feels good and safe;
but Father, I kid myself that I am loving you when
I am loving myself.

Help me—I call myself Christian. I claim
to be one of your special people. Free me from
feeling special privilege and not special
responsibility. Free me from loving religion
instead of you.

Amen.

Quittin' Time

O God,

> For the clock that alarms,
> for the lights that come on,
> for the heat from the furnace,
> for soap and toothpaste,
> for food on the table,

> > > Thank you.

> For the tools of my work,
> for my place of work.
> for others who work with me,
> for others' depending on me,

> > > Thank you.

> For smiles,
> for satisfaction of good work,
> for challenges, and
> for "quittin' time,"

> > > Thank you.

Jim Daughdrill is Secretary of Stewardship for the Presbyterian Church in the United States. He was pastor of St. Andrew's Presbyterian Church, Little Rock, Arkansas, and prior to his ordination to the ministry was president of Kingston Mills, Inc., Cartersville, Georgia. He was a member of the Young Presidents' Organization—an international group of company presidents under forty years of age, whose companies have annual sales over five million dollars.

72 73 74 10 9 8 7 6 5 4 3 2 1